TIME TRAVELING TO
1944

CELEBRATING A SPECIAL YEAR

TIME TRAVELING TO 1944

Author
Charles A. Thompson

Design
Gonçalo Sousa

January 2024
ISBN: 9798874424466

Surprise!

Dear reader, thank you so much for purchasing my book!

To make this book more (much more!) affordable, the images are all black & white, but I've created a special gift for you!

You can now have access, for FREE, to the PDF version of this book with the original images!

Keep in mind that some are originally black and white, but some are colored.

Go to page 105 and follow the instructions to download it.

I hope you enjoy it!

Contents

Chapter I: News & Current Events 1944

Leading Events

D-Day Invasion: A Pivotal Moment in World War II - June 6th

American assault troops in a landing craft during the Normandy Invasion

The D-Day Invasion, codenamed Operation Neptune and a crucial part of Operation Overlord, marked a turning point in World War II. This meticulously planned operation, the largest seaborne invasion in history, initiated the liberation of France and Western Europe, significantly contributing to the eventual Allied victory on the Western Front. Allied forces, led by Major General Dwight D. Eisenhower, faced formidable German defenses commanded by Field Marshal Erwin Rommel. The invasion's success hinged on a complex strategy, including Operation Bodyguard, a deception plan to mislead the Germans about the invasion's timing and location. The initial date was postponed by 24 hours due to adverse weather, underlining the operation's reliance on specific lunar phases, tides, and times.

The operation commenced with an airborne assault involving 24,000 troops from the United States, Britain, and Canada. Following this, the amphibious landings began at 06:30 on a 50-mile stretch of Normandy, segmented into

Overview of the Normandy Invasion

Utah, Omaha, Gold, Juno, and Sword sectors. Despite the challenging conditions, including strong winds and heavily fortified German positions with gun emplacements, mines, and various obstacles, the Allied forces managed to establish a beachhead.

The assault faced intense resistance, particularly at Omaha Beach, noted for its high cliffs and heavy casualties. The Allies engaged in rigorous combat, clearing several towns and disabling key German defenses. Although the initial objectives were not fully achieved on D-Day, with important locations like Caen remaining contested until late July, the operation secured a crucial foothold. This initial success was vital, despite the heavy price: German casualties were estimated at 4,000 to 9,000, and the Allies suffered over 10,000 casualties, including 4,414 confirmed dead.

Operation Bagration: Soviet Blitz Cripples German Army - June 22nd

Operation Bagration, a critical Soviet offensive in World War II, inflicted the largest defeat in German military history on Army Group Centre. Coinciding with Operation Overlord in the west, this campaign forced Germany to fight on two major fronts. The Soviets annihilated 28 of 34 divisions of Army Group Centre, causing about 450,000 German casualties and trapping 300,000 in the Courland Pocket. The Red Army's assault began with the aim of encircling and destroying German forces in Byelorussia. Rapid advancements led to the decimation of

Soviet infantry in action during Bagration

the German 4th Army and significant portions of the Third Panzer and Ninth Armies. This swift action facilitated the encirclement and eventual liberation of Minsk, marking the end of effective German resistance in the region.

This operation was notable for the successful implementation of Soviet deep battle and maskirovka (deception) tactics, albeit with substantial losses. By diverting German reserves from the Lublin–Brest and Lvov–Sandomierz areas, the Soviets paved the way for further offensives, advancing to the Vistula river and Warsaw. This positioned Soviet forces within striking distance of Berlin, aligning with their strategy of striking deep into enemy territory.

Operation Bagration reshaped the Eastern Front, significantly weakening German forces and altering the balance of power, marking a crucial turning point in the war.

An imposing column of Soviet armor advances against the retreating Germans

Warsaw Uprising: Heroic Yet Tragic Struggle Against Nazis - August 1st

The Warsaw Uprising, a significant yet catastrophic effort by the Polish underground resistance Home Army, aimed to liberate Warsaw from German occupation. As the largest European resistance operation during World War II,

German soldiers fighting the Polish resistance in Warsaw

it began as part of Operation Tempest, coinciding with the Soviet Lublin–Brest Offensive.

The uprising's goals were to oust the Germans from Warsaw and assert Polish sovereignty before the Soviet-backed Polish Committee of National Liberation could take control. Motivated by a deep desire for justice after years of oppressive German occupation, and spurred by imminent threats of mass German round-ups, the Polish resistance embarked on this daring endeavor. However, the uprising was met with severe challenges. The nearby Red Army, despite expectations, did not provide support, allowing the Germans to crush the Polish

Resistance fighter armed with a K pattern flamethrower

resistance. This lack of Soviet support, as revealed by recent scholarship and declassified documents, reflected Stalin's broader ambitions in Eastern Europe, contributing to the onset of Cold War tensions.

The uprising endured for 63 days with minimal outside assistance, leading to devastating casualties. Around 16,000 Polish resistance fighters were killed, and 6,000 more were critically wounded. Civilian losses were horrific, with estimates ranging from 150,000 to 200,000, including mass executions. The defeat not only resulted in extensive destruction in urban Poland but also highlighted the clash between Polish democratic aspirations and Stalin's plans for Sovietizing postwar Central and Eastern Europe.

Paris Liberated: Joyous Victory Over Nazi Forces - August 25th

Crowds of French patriots line the Champs, after Paris was liberated

The Liberation of Paris marked a key moment in World War II, ending Nazi Germany's occupation of the French capital, which began following the 1940 Armistice. This joyous victory unfolded over several days, culminating in the city's liberation from German control.

The battle for Paris commenced with the French Forces of the Interior, the armed wing of the French Resistance, initiating an uprising against the German garrison. Their efforts were bolstered by the approaching US Third Army, led by General George S. Patton. In a significant move on the night of August 24, elements of

A British AFPU photographer kisses a child

General Philippe Leclerc de Hauteclocque's 2nd French Armored Division penetrated Paris, reaching the Hôtel de Ville just before midnight.
The following morning saw the arrival of the main contingents of the 2nd Armored Division, along with the US 4th Infantry Division and other allied units, effectively signaling the liberation of Paris. The German garrison, commanded by Dietrich von Choltitz, capitulated, with von Choltitz surrendering at the Hôtel Le Meurice, which had been designated the new French headquarters.

General de Gaulle and his entourage proudly stroll down the Champs Élysées

General Charles de Gaulle, a prominent figure in the French military and head of the Provisional Government of the French Republic, arrived to take control of Paris. This marked a significant turning point, not only in the liberation of France but also in boosting the morale of the Allied forces.

Battle of Leyte Gulf: History's Largest Naval Battle - October 23rd-26th

The Battle of Leyte Gulf, recognized as the largest naval battle in both World War II and history, involved over 200,000 naval personnel. Fought near the Philippine islands of Leyte, Samar, and Luzon, this battle was a fundamental part of the Leyte invasion, aiming to cut off Japan from its

USS Princeton (CVL-23) burning, bombed near the Philippines

Southeast Asian colonies, essential for industrial and oil resources.

The battle, occurring in late October 1944, pitted combined American and Australian forces against the Imperial Japanese Navy (IJN). At this stage, Japan's naval capability, especially in terms of capital ships, was significantly diminished compared to the Allies' amassed aircraft carriers in the Pacific. Nevertheless, the IJN committed nearly all its remaining major vessels to counter the Allied invasion, only to be repulsed by the US Navy's Third and Seventh Fleets.

Comprising four main engagements – the Battle of the Sibuyan Sea, the Battle of Surigao Strait, the Battle off Cape Engaño, and the Battle off Samar – along with several smaller actions, the battle marked the first instance of organized kamikaze attacks by Japanese aircraft. Notably, it was also the last historical naval battle involving battleships.

The aftermath of the Battle of Leyte Gulf was devastating for the Japanese Navy, which suffered significant losses and was effectively incapacitated for the remainder of the war.

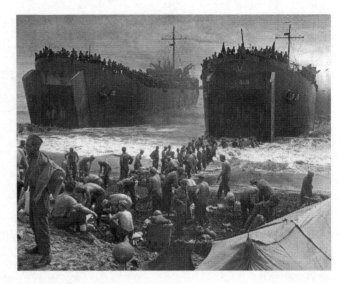

U.S. landing ships, tanks (LSTs), on the beach at Leyte Island

Other Major Events

Anzio Landing: Allies' Strategic Advance in Europe – Jan. 25th – Jun. 5th

The Battle of Anzio, a significant segment of the Italian Campaign in World War II, began with Operation Shingle, an Allied amphibious landing aimed at outflanking German forces at the Winter Line to facilitate an attack on Rome. Led initially by Major General John P. Lucas of the U.S. Army, this operation was challenged by German and Italian Repubblica Sociale Italiana forces.

The landing's success hinged on surprise and rapid movement inland, with any delay risking entrapment by enemy forces. Despite achieving complete surprise and even reaching the outskirts of Rome with

US Army troops landing at Anzio in Operation Shingle

minimal opposition, Lucas hesitated to advance, preferring to consolidate his position in anticipation of a counterattack. This delay allowed Field Marshal Albert Kesselring, the German commander,

Tanks debark from LST US 77 in Anzio, bolstering VI Corps

to fortify a defensive ring around the beachhead, bombarding the Allies relentlessly and flooding the marshland to hinder their progress. After a month of intense but inconclusive combat, Lucas was replaced by Major General Lucian Truscott.

The Allied breakout occurred in May, but instead of cutting off the German Tenth Army at Monte Cassino, they moved northwest towards Rome on Clark's orders, capturing it on June 4, 1944. This strategy allowed the German Tenth Army to retreat and regroup, continuing their defensive campaign from the formidable Gothic Line. This battle, while culminating in the strategic capture of Rome, also illustrated the complexities and challenges of Allied decision-making in the Italian theater.

Exercise Tiger: Amphibious Tragedy's Crucial Lessons - April 27th

Exercise Tiger, a crucial but disastrous rehearsal for D-Day's Utah Beach landing, culminated in a catastrophe on the night of April 27th, off Devon's Slapton Sands, resulting in 946 American servicemen's deaths.
In 1943, to simulate the Normandy coastline, over 3,000 South Devon residents were evacuated, transforming the peaceful River Dart area into a military hub with landing craft, ships, and temporary structures.

American troops land in England for 'Exercise Tiger', pre-D-Day rehearsal

The exercise, aimed at realism, began on April 22nd, 1944, with soldiers, tanks, and equipment deployed along the coast. Tragically, German E-boats infiltrated the area, sinking two landing ships and damaging a third. Many soldiers, untrained in using life vests, drowned or succumbed to hypothermia. The ensuing live-firing exercise on Slapton beach added to the casualties due to friendly fire from naval bombardment.

The scale of the tragedy was concealed to maintain morale, with details emerging only post-war. Despite the significant loss, Exercise Tiger

American troops are brought ashore by their LCVP boat during Exercise Tiger

played a crucial role in the successful Utah Beach landing, with fewer casualties experienced in the actual operation than during the rehearsal. This underscored the exercise's importance in preparing troops for D-Day, albeit at a great cost.

Exercise Tiger's legacy extends beyond Slapton, as Devon's Woolacombe Bay also served as a training ground for amphibious assaults, highlighting the region's strategic role in the Allies' preparations for the historic Normandy landings.

GI Bill Enacted: Transforming Post-War America - June 22nd

President Roosevelt signs the G.I. Bill into law

The G.I. Bill, or the Servicemen's Readjustment Act of 1944, significantly transformed post-war America by offering a range of benefits to World War II veterans. Spearheaded by the American Legion and championed by John H. Stelle, the bill was a bipartisan triumph. It diverged from President Roosevelt's initial focus on employment, shifting towards educational opportunities after insights from Anna M. Rosenberg's reports on G.I.'s postwar expectations.

The bill provided immediate financial rewards, including low-cost mortgages, low-interest loans, unemployment compensation, and funding for education and vocational training. Eligibility extended to veterans who served at least 90 days during the war and were honorably discharged.

By 1956, the G.I. Bill had facilitated education and training for 7.8 million

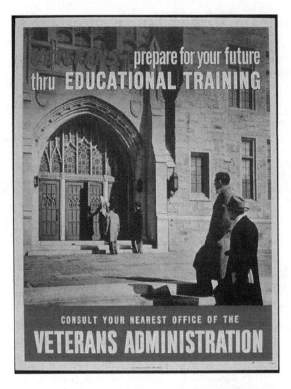

A government poster informing soldiers about the
G.I. Bill

veterans, bolstering the U.S. human capital and contributing to long-term economic growth. However, it faced criticism for exacerbating racial wealth disparities in the Jim Crow era. The original bill expired in 1956, but its legacy continued with the Post-9/11 Veterans Educational Assistance Act of 2008 and the Forever GI Bill of 2017, extending benefits to newer generations of veterans.

Bretton Woods: Shaping the New Global Economy - July 1st-22nd

U.N. Monetary Conference

The Bretton Woods Conference, held in New Hampshire, United States, was a decisive moment in shaping the post-World War II global economy. Attended by 730 delegates from 44 allied nations, the conference led to the creation of the International Monetary Fund (IMF) and the International Bank for Reconstruction and Development (IBRD), later a part of the World Bank group.

Delegates at the Bretton Woods Conference

The conference established the Bretton Woods system, setting the framework for international financial and commercial relations. The IMF aimed to promote stable exchange rates and facilitate financial flows, while the IBRD focused on post-war reconstruction and economic development.

Key outcomes included an adjustably pegged foreign exchange rate system, pegged to gold, and provisions for member countries to regulate capital flows. Countries pledged currency convertibility for trade and other transactions, with the IMF overseeing adjustments in exchange rates and managing member contributions.

Membership in the IBRD was conditioned on IMF membership, with voting power in both institutions based on countries' financial contributions. This conference laid the foundation for modern financial institutions and systems, significantly influencing the global economic landscape.

Belgrade Offensive: Pivotal Step in Balkans' Liberation – Sept. 15th – Nov. 24th

The Belgrade Offensive, a crucial military operation from September to November 1944, was instrumental in liberating Belgrade from German control during World War II. This joint effort involved the Soviet Red Army, Yugoslav Partisans, and the Bulgarian Army, marking a significant step in the Balkans' liberation.

Strategically coordinated by Soviet and Yugoslav leaders, including Josip Broz Tito and Joseph Stalin, the operation aimed to end German

Destroyed Soviet Red Army T-34/85 tank in Belgrade

occupation in Serbia and establish control over Belgrade, a key Balkan stronghold. It also sought to disrupt German communication lines between Greece and Hungary.

The offensive's main thrust was led by the Soviet 3rd Ukrainian

Belgrade is liberated by the Red Army and Yugoslav Partisans

Front and the Yugoslav 1st Army Corps. Concurrently, the Bulgarian 2nd Army and Yugoslav XIII Army Corps engaged in the south, while the 2nd Ukrainian Front advanced from the Yugoslav-Bulgarian border, intensifying pressure on German forces.

This comprehensive campaign, marked by cooperation among the Soviet, Yugoslav, and Bulgarian forces, successfully breached German defenses in the region, resulting in the strategic capture of Belgrade and a significant weakening of German influence in the Balkans.

Political Events

Iceland's Independence: A New National Era Begins - June 17th

Icelanders celebrating independence at Þingvellir

The Icelandic independence movement, a peaceful endeavor from its inception in the post-Napoleonic era to its culmination in 1944, was characterized by several key factors. The geographical distance of Iceland from Copenhagen, Iceland's culturally homogeneous population, and the accommodating nature of Danish responses to Icelandic demands contributed significantly to the movement's non-violent nature. Denmark's respect for Icelandic culture and reluctance to bear the costs of suppressing the independence movement further facilitated a peaceful transition.

In 1874, Iceland was granted home rule by Denmark, a milestone that came a thousand years after its first settlement. Subsequent constitutional revisions and the establishment of an Icelandic minister underscored this growing autonomy. The 1918 Act of Union, ratified overwhelmingly by Icelandic voters, recognized Iceland as a sovereign state in personal union with Denmark, maintaining the Danish king as a symbolic figurehead.

The peaceful path to full independence culminated in 1944 during the Nazi occupation of Denmark, when Icelanders voted overwhelmingly to establish the Republic of Iceland, severing all political ties with Denmark and fully asserting their independence.

Dumbarton Oaks: Paving the Way for the United Nations – Aug. 21st – Oct. 7th

Participants of the conference

The Dumbarton Oaks Conference, held in Washington, D.C, was a significant step towards establishing the United Nations. Led by the "Four Policemen" – the United States, the United Kingdom, the Soviet Union, and China – this conference aimed to create a framework for an international organization dedicated to maintaining world peace and security.

This conference, fulfilling a key aspect of the 1943 Moscow Declaration, saw deliberations among delegations from these major powers. Notable representatives included Sir Alexander Cadogan from the UK, Andrei Gromyko

Dumbarton Oaks in Washington, D.C., was the location of the conference.

from the Soviet Union, Wellington Koo from China, and Edward Stettinius Jr. from the U.S. The conference was chaired by Stettinius, with U.S. Secretary of State Cordell Hull delivering the opening address. Discussions occurred in two phases due to Soviet reluctance to directly engage with the Chinese. The first phase involved the Soviet Union, the UK, and the U.S., and the second phase included China, the UK, and the U.S. The outcomes of the Dumbarton Oaks Conference laid the groundwork for the formation of the United Nations, a fundamental organization in global diplomacy and international relations.

King Michael I of Romania

King Michael's Bold Coup: Romania Swings to Allies - August 23rd

King Michael I of Romania led a transformative coup, famously known as the Act of 23 August in Romanian historiography, significantly altering Romania's role in World War II. Initially perceived as a figurehead, he collaborated with the army and pro-Allied politicians to overthrow the government of Ion Antonescu, who had aligned Romania with Nazi Germany. During a crucial meeting, King Michael urged Antonescu to exit the war and seek an armistice with the Allies and Soviets. Antonescu's refusal to agree triggered the coup, leading

Troops of the 3rd Ukrainian Front entering Bucharest

to his arrest. That night, King Michael took to the radio to announce the government's overthrow and his intention to accept an armistice with the Allied Powers and the Soviet Union.

In response, the Germans attempted to reverse the situation through military action. However, the Romanian forces, including the First and Second Armies, along with remnants of the Third and Fourth Armies, were ordered by the king to defend against German attacks, realigning Romania's battered armies with the Allies.

Roosevelt's Historic Win: A Fourth Term in U.S. Election - November 7th

Election night

In the 1944 United States elections, President Franklin D. Roosevelt secured a historic victory, winning an unprecedented fourth term amidst the final stages of World War II. Roosevelt, already the longest-serving

I WANT YOU F.D.R.

STAY AND FINISH THE JOB!

INDEPENDENT VOTERS COMMITTEE OF THE ARTS and SCIENCES for ROOSEVELT

Poster from 1944 presidential campaign

President in U.S. history, defeated Republican nominee Thomas E. Dewey in a landslide, garnering 432 electoral votes to Dewey's 99. Despite opposition from groups like the Texas Regulars, who opposed Roosevelt's New Deal and his policies on African Americans, his success was overwhelming. The Democratic Party maintained its majority in both Congressional chambers. In the Senate, Democrats held control despite losing some seats, and in the House of Representatives, they expanded their slim majority by gaining 22 seats. Democrats also gained three governorships.

The election served as a referendum on Roosevelt's leadership during the war. With significant Allied victories, including the fall of fascist Italy and the Normandy landings, public support rallied around the Democrats. Sadly, Roosevelt passed away in April 1945, shortly after his fourth inauguration.

Other Notable Events

Hartford Circus Tragedy: Devastating Fire Shocks Nation - July 6th

The Hartford circus fire, one of the worst fire disasters in U.S. history, struck Hartford, Connecticut, during a Ringling Bros. and Barnum & Bailey Circus performance. The tragedy, unfolding before an audience of 6,000 to 8,000 people, resulted in at least 167 deaths and over 700 injuries, making it the deadliest disaster in Connecticut's history.

The Hartford Circus Fire

The fire ignited on the tent's southwest sidewall shortly after the lion act, during The Flying Wallendas' performance. Circus bandleader Merle Evans, first to spot the flames, signaled distress by playing "The Stars and Stripes Forever". Amidst a power outage that rendered Ringmaster Fred Bradna's calls for orderly evacuation inaudible, panic ensued. Ushers initially tried to douse the fire with water jugs and tear down burning canvas sections but soon shifted to aiding the frantic evacuation.

This catastrophic event shocked the nation, highlighting the urgent need for improved safety measures in public entertainment venues.

Photo # NH 96823 Damage at Port Chicago, Ca. View looking north toward pier.

Damage at the Port Chicago Pier after the explosion

Port Chicago Catastrophe: A Blow to Military and Racial Justice - July 17th

The Port Chicago disaster, a catastrophic munitions explosion on the SS E. A. Bryan in 1944 at Port Chicago, California, profoundly impacted military and racial justice in the United States. The explosion killed 320 sailors and civilians, and injured 390 others, with two-thirds of the casualties being African American sailors. This tragedy underscored the racial inequities in the military, as these sailors were assigned the dangerous task of loading ammunition under unsafe conditions.

African American sailors preparing 5-inch shells for packing

The disaster led to the Port Chicago Mutiny, where hundreds of servicemen, protesting unsafe working conditions, refused to load munitions. Fifty of these men, known as the "Port Chicago 50", were controversially convicted of mutiny, sentenced to prison and hard labor, and dishonorably discharged. Although most were released by early 1946, the incident raised significant questions about the fairness and legality of the trials.

The widespread publicity and public outcry over this case contributed to the U.S. Navy's decision to desegregate its forces starting in February 1946, marking a decisive moment in the fight against racial discrimination. In 1994, the Port Chicago Naval Magazine National Memorial was established to honor those lost in the disaster.

Majdanek Camp Liberated: Exposing Holocaust Horrors - July 23rd

Majdanek, also known as Lublin, was a Nazi concentration and extermination camp established by the SS on the outskirts of Lublin, Poland, during World War II. Among the largest Nazi camps, it included seven gas chambers, two wooden gallows, and 227 structures. Originally intended for forced labor, Majdanek became a site of industrial-scale extermination

Soviet soldiers inspect the ovens at Majdanek

during Operation Reinhard, the plan to annihilate Polish Jews.

Operational from October 1941 until July 1944, the camp was captured nearly intact, thanks to the rapid advance of the Soviet Red Army. This prevented the SS from destroying evidence of war crimes, including the infrastructure of genocide. Known locally as "Majdanek" due to its proximity to the Majdan Tatarski ghetto, the camp was later preserved as a museum, with its crematorium ovens and gas chambers intact.

In 2005, Tomasz Kranz, director of the Research Department of the State Museum at Majdanek, provided an official estimate of 78,000 victims, including 59,000 Jews.

Tragic Capture of Anne Frank: A Stark Reminder of War - August 4th

Annelies Marie Frank, a German-born Jewish girl, became an emblem of the Holocaust through her diary, which vividly captured her life in hiding from Nazi persecution. Born in Frankfurt, Germany, Anne and her family moved to Amsterdam in 1934. After Adolf Hitler's rise to power and the Nazi occupation of the Netherlands, the Frank family found themselves trapped

Anne Frank in May 1942

in Amsterdam. In July 1942, as Jewish persecutions intensified, they went into hiding in a concealed attic behind a bookcase in Otto Frank's workplace.

Anne's diary, a birthday gift, became her solace and witness to their life in hiding until their tragic capture by the Gestapo on August 4th, 1944. Anne and her sister Margot were later transferred to Bergen-Belsen concentration camp, where they perished, likely from typhus, in early 1945.

Otto Frank, the sole survivor

The Frank family

of the family, discovered that Anne's diary had been preserved. Fulfilling her aspiration to be a writer, he published it in 1947. "The Diary of a Young Girl" has since become a poignant symbol of the horrors of war, translated into over 70 languages and touching hearts worldwide.

Tuvan Annexation: Soviet Expansion Redraws Borders - October 11th

The Soviet Union annexed Tuva, a territory with a rich and varied history, further expanding Soviet borders. This annexation, approved by Tuva's Little Khural (parliament) but without a public referendum, shrouded the event in obscurity. Salchak Toka, leader of the Tuvan People's Revolutionary Party, became the de facto ruler as the First Secretary of the Tuvan Communist Party, a position he held until his death in 1973.

Initially designated as the Tuvan Autonomous Oblast, Tuva later became

Decree on the entry of Tuva into the
USSR

Salchak Toka

the Tuvan Autonomous Soviet Socialist Republic in 1961. The Soviet Union
kept Tuva isolated from the outside world for nearly fifty years. Tuva's history
is marked by various dominions, from Scythian presence in the 9th century
BC, through successive Turkic khanates, Mongol-led regimes, and Manchu-
led Qing dynasty, to slow Russian colonization and eventual incorporation
into Russia in the 20th century.

Tuva's integration into the Russian Empire, the Soviet Union, and
ultimately the Russian Federation in 1992, reflects its strategic and historical
significance in the region, with its borders remaining largely unchanged
throughout this tumultuous history.

Chapter II: Crime & Punishment 1944

Oradour-sur-Glane Horror: Emblem of Nazi Brutality - June 10th

What was left in the ruins of Oradour-sur-Glane

The village of Oradour-sur-Glane in Nazi-occupied France became a symbol of Nazi brutality when a German Waffen-SS company massacred 643 civilians, including men, women, and children, as collective punishment for Resistance activities in the area. This horrific act was in retaliation for the capture and execution of Waffen SS Sturmbannfuhrer Helmut Kämpfe. The Germans executed everyone present in the village, including those passing through, with men shot in the legs and burned in barns, and women and children herded into a church that was set ablaze.

Among the victims were 17 Spanish citizens, 8 Italians, and 3 Poles. Only six people miraculously escaped, with the last survivor, Robert Hébras, passing away in 2023 at the age of 97. The village remains a ruin, preserved as a memorial and museum by order of President Charles de Gaulle, while a new village was built nearby after the war.

Tragic Fate of George Stinney: Youngest Executed in Modern U.S. - June 16th

George Stinney mugshot

George Junius Stinney Jr., an African American boy, became the youngest American in the 20th century to be sentenced to death and executed following a controversial and later vacated conviction. At 14, Stinney was wrongfully convicted for the murders of two young girls, Betty June Binnicker, 11, and Mary Emma Thames, 7, in Alcolu, South Carolina. His trial and execution by electric chair were later scrutinized for their unfairness. In 2004, a re-examination of Stinney's case was initiated, spearheaded by several individuals and the Northeastern University School of Law. This led to a significant legal reversal in 2014, when a South Carolina court vacated Stinney's murder conviction, seventy years post-execution. The court ruled that he had not received a fair trial, officially acknowledging his wrongful execution.

Wola District Bloodshed: Dark Chapter in Warsaw Uprising - August 5th-12th

The Wola massacre, a harrowing episode during the Warsaw Uprising, saw the systematic killing of 40,000 to 50,000 Poles in Warsaw's Wola district by the Waffen-SS, the Azerbaijani Legion, and RONA forces. Ordered by Heinrich Himmler to quash the uprising, this atrocity involved the mass execution of civilians, resistance fighters, and hospital patients, including children and the elderly. Perpetrated primarily by the Dirlewanger Brigade and the "RONA" Kaminski Brigade, the brutality included torture, sexual assault, and the use of dogs to find survivors for execution. Bodies were piled and burned to destroy evidence. Contrary to German expectations of demoralizing the Polish resistance, the massacre only intensified their resolve. The fierce response prolonged the uprising, with the Germans taking another two months to regain control of Warsaw. This dark chapter highlights the extreme brutality faced by the Polish population during World War II.

A column of Polish women with children being led by German troops

Ardeatine's Grim Retribution: Nazi Atrocities in Italy - March 24th

The Ardeatine massacre was a horrendous event during the Second World War, where German occupation troops executed 335 civilians and political prisoners in Rome as retaliation for the Via Rasella attack against the SS Police Regiment Bozen. This mass killing, carried out at the Ardeatine Caves, marked one of the most horrific atrocities committed on

German troops and Italian soldiers round up civilians

35

Italian soil during the war. In remembrance of this dark chapter, the site has been declared a Memorial Cemetery and National Monument, visited daily by those paying respects.

Each year, a solemn state commemoration is held, attended by senior officials of the Italian Republic. During this ceremony, the names of all 335 victims are called out, symbolizing their individual identities and the collective loss endured by the community.

Auschwitz Revolt: Defiance in the Face of Despair - October 7th

Auschwitz I survivors, entrance, January 1945, under 'Arbeit macht frei' ("Work sets you free") sign

In a courageous act of defiance at Auschwitz-Birkenau, prisoners assigned to Crematorium IV revolted upon realizing they were slated for execution. For months, Jewish women like Ester Wajcblum, Ella Gärtner, and Regina Safirsztain had smuggled gunpowder from a munitions factory in the camp to the resistance. They discreetly transported the gunpowder, which was then passed to Róza Robota and other members of the Sonderkommando, a squad forced to work in the crematoria. Their plan was to destroy the gas chambers and incite an uprising.

The revolt, sparked by impending liquidation of the squad, saw fierce resistance from the Sonderkommando. However, the Germans brutally crushed the mutiny, resulting in the death of nearly 450 prisoners during and after the revolt. Subsequently, four Jewish women involved

Children liberated in the Auschwitz concentration camp, 1945

in the explosives supply were executed, marking a poignant moment of resistance amidst the horrors of the Holocaust.

Chapter III: Entertainment 1944

Silver Screen

Going My Way

Top Film of 1944: Going My Way

"Going My Way," a 1944 American musical comedy-drama, directed by the adept Leo McCarey, features the indomitable Bing Crosby alongside Barry Fitzgerald. The film, penned by Frank Butler and Frank Cavett, spins a tale of generational transition within a parish, with Crosby's youthful priest rejuvenating an old veteran's domain. This cinematic piece not only showcases Crosby's vocal prowess through five enchanting songs but also includes performances by Risë Stevens of the Metropolitan Opera and the Robert Mitchell Boys Choir.

This film emerged as the highest-grossing movie of 1944, enchanting audiences and sweeping the Academy Awards with seven wins, including Best Picture. Crosby's stellar performance, hailed as his career's zenith by Bosley Crowther of The New York Times, alongside Fitzgerald's heartwarming act, elevated the film to a critical and commercial triumph. It's a film where Crosby's harmonious melodies, like "Going My Way" and "Swing on a Star," blend seamlessly with Fitzgerald's compelling screen presence.

"Going My Way" not only solidified Crosby's status as a box-office titan but also resonated so profoundly that a copy was presented to Pope Pius XII. Its sequel, "The Bells of St. Mary's," followed in 1945. Embraced for its endearing sentimentality yet critiqued for an excess of sweetness, the film holds a revered place in cinematic history, symbolizing the golden era of Hollywood musicals.

Remaining Top 3

Meet Me in St. Louis

Meet Me in St. Louis

"Meet Me in St. Louis," a 1944 Metro-Goldwyn-Mayer Christmas musical, unfolds in a series of seasonal vignettes, portraying a year in the life of the Smith family in the lead-up to the 1904 Louisiana Purchase Exposition. Directed by Vincente Minnelli and starring the illustrious Judy Garland alongside Margaret O'Brien, Mary Astor, and others, the film delves into the charming family dynamics and societal nuances of early 20th century St. Louis. Adapted from Sally Benson's "The Kensington Stories," this cinematic treasure became a critical and commercial success, standing as MGM's most successful musical of the 1940s. Garland's renditions of "The Trolley Song" and "Have Yourself a Merry Little Christmas" became instant classics, contributing to the film's four Academy Award nominations.

In 1994, its cultural, historical, and aesthetic significance was recognized by its selection for preservation in the U.S. National Film Registry. The film was placed 10th on the American Film Institute's list of Greatest Movie Musicals.

"Two Girls and a Sailor" & "Bathing Beauty"

Two Girls and a Sailor

Bathing Beauty

"Two Girls and a Sailor," a 1944 American musical set during World War II, and "Bathing Beauty," a Technicolor romantic comedy of the same year, both captivated audiences, tying for third place in the highest-grossing films of 1944.

Directed by Richard Thorpe, "Two Girls and a Sailor" stars Van Johnson, June Allyson, and Gloria DeHaven in a story about two singing sisters who create a canteen to entertain military members, with support from a mysterious donor. It features celebrity performances, including Jimmy Durante's "Inka Dinka Doo," earning an Academy Award nomination for Best Original Screenplay.

"Bathing Beauty," directed by George Sidney and starring Red Skelton and Esther Williams, intertwines the tale of songwriter Steve Elliot, played by Skelton, preparing to marry Caroline Brooks, a college swimming instructor portrayed by Williams. As both plan to leave their careers for marriage, Steve faces a dilemma with a New York producer hiring him for a water ballet show. Initially titled "Mr. Co-Ed," the film was refocused to highlight Williams, leading to its iconic title and status.

 Top 1944 Movies at The Domestic Box Office (the-numbers.com)

Rank	Title	Date	Total Gross
1	Going My Way	May 3, 1944	$16,300,000
2	Meet Me in St. Louis	Nov 28, 1944	$12,800,000
3	Two Girls and a Sailor	Apr 27, 1944	$3,500,000
4	Bathing Beauty	Jun 27, 1944	$3,500,000
5	Wilson	Aug 1, 1944	$2,000,000
6	Snow White and the Seven Dwarfs	Feb 22, 1944	$1,400,000

Other Film Releases

The cinematic landscape of 1944, a pivotal year in Hollywood's golden era, was marked by films that, while not dominating the box office, evolved into timeless cult classics. Among these, "Double Indemnity," "Laura," "Gaslight," "Arsenic and Old Lace," "To Have and Have Not," and "Lifeboat" stood out for their narrative ingenuity and enduring appeal.

"Double Indemnity," directed by the illustrious Billy Wilder, redefined the film noir genre with its tale of lust, betrayal, and murder. The electric

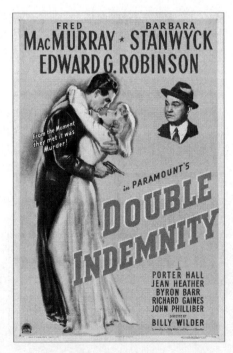

Double Indemnity

chemistry between Fred MacMurray and Barbara Stanwyck, coupled with Wilder's masterful direction and Raymond Chandler's sharp screenplay, crafted a cinematic masterpiece. Its narrative sophistication and moral ambiguity continue to influence filmmakers and captivate audiences.

Otto Preminger's "Laura" is another noir classic, presenting a captivating plot where detective Mark McPherson investigates the apparent murder of the enchanting Laura Hunt, portrayed by Gene Tierney. The narrative takes a spellbinding twist when Laura, presumed dead, reappears, unraveling a deeper web of romance and mystery, enhanced by the film's haunting score and elegant cinematography.

In "Gaslight," directed by George Cukor, Ingrid Bergman delivers a stellar performance, portraying a woman on the brink of insanity. This psychological thriller, exploring manipulation and mental cruelty, has contributed the term 'gaslighting' to the modern lexicon and stands as a significant work in both film history and social commentary.

The Frank Capra-directed "Arsenic and Old Lace," adapted from a successful

Laura

Gaslight

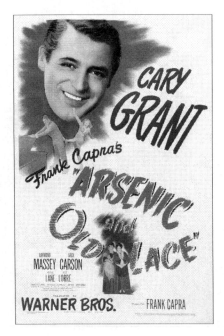

Arsenic and Old Lace   To Have and Have Not

Broadway play, offered a delightful blend of dark comedy and farce. Cary Grant's comedic genius shone through in this macabre tale of murderous aunts, blending humor with a touch of the sinister, ensuring its status as a beloved classic.

Howard Hawks' "To Have and Have Not" marked the beginning of the legendary on- and off-screen partnership between Humphrey Bogart and Lauren Bacall. Set against the backdrop of World War II, the film combined romance, adventure, and espionage, with Bacall's sultry presence and the couple's palpable chemistry making it an unforgettable cinematic experience.

Lastly, Alfred Hitchcock's "Lifeboat," a wartime drama set entirely in a lifeboat, showcased the director's prowess in creating suspense and psychological drama in confined spaces. The film's exploration of human nature and survival, along with Tallulah Bankhead's commanding performance, underscored Hitchcock's ability to captivate audiences with minimalistic yet powerful storytelling.

Lifeboat

These six films from 1944, each unique in their themes and execution, have transcended their initial release to become cultural touchstones. Their exploration of complex characters, innovative storytelling, and stylistic flair not only enriched the cinematic arts but also left an indelible mark on popular culture. From noir to comedy, romance to thriller, these films represent a cross-section of an industry at its creative zenith, continuing to inspire and entertain generations of moviegoers.

The 1st Golden Globe Awards – Thursday, January 20th, 1944

🏆 Winners

Best Performance in a Motion Picture –
Drama – Actor:
Paul Lukas (Watch on the Rhine)

Best Performance in a Motion Picture –
Drama – Actress:
Jennifer Jones (The Song of Bernadette)

Best Performance in a Motion Picture –
Supporting Actor:
Akim Tamiroff (For Whom the Bell Tolls)

Best Performance in a Motion Picture –
Supporting Actress:
Katina Paxinou (For Whom the Bell Tolls)

Best Supporting Performance in a Motion
Picture – Actor:
John Huston (The Cardinal)

Best Picture – Drama:
The Song of Bernadette

 In 1944, the British Academy Film Awards (nowadays, called the
BAFTA Film Awards) did not exist.

The 16th Academy Awards – Thursday, March 2nd, 1944 - Grauman's Chinese Theatre, Hollywood, Los Angeles, California

Outstanding Motion Picture: Casablanca
– Hal B. Wallis for Warner Bros.

Best Director:
Michael Curtiz (Casablanca)

Best Actor: Paul Lukas (Watch on the Rhine)
Best Actress: Jennifer Jones (The Song of Bernadette)

Best Supporting Actor:
Charles Coburn (The More the Merrier)

Best Supporting Actress:
Katina Paxinou (For Whom the Bell Tolls)

Best Original Screenplay: Princess
O'Rourke – Norman Krasna

Best Original Motion Picture Story:
The Human Comedy – William Saroyan

Best Cinematography, Black-and-White:
The Song of Bernadette – Arthur C. Miller

Best Cinematography, Color: Phantom of the
Opera – Hal Mohr and W. Howard Greene

Top of the Charts

Top Album: "The King Cole Trio" by The King Cole Trio

The King Cole Trio

In 1944, the jazz world was graced with "The King Cole Trio," the debut commercial recordings of Nat King Cole and his trio, released by Capitol Records. These albums marked a significant milestone in Cole's illustrious career as a jazz pianist and vocalist. Originally issued in sets of 78 r.p.m. records, they captured the refined artistry and smooth sound that would become Cole's trademark.

Featuring a blend of jazz and pop elements, these recordings showcased Cole's exceptional talent and versatility, setting the stage for his future success. The album's release was a historic moment, as it became the first-ever No. 1 on the Billboard album chart when it was first published on March 24, 1945.

Even today, "The King Cole Trio" is celebrated for its pioneering contribution to jazz music and for cementing Nat King Cole's status as one of the genre's most influential and enduring figures.

Best Albums and Singles

In 1944, a year deeply marked by World War II, music provided a much-needed escape and solace. The era's sound was a rich tapestry, blending the rhythmic innovations of jazz with the emotive power of vocal performances. Tommy Dorsey, Glenn Miller, Benny Goodman, and Artie Shaw's "Up

Swing" brought together the giants of swing, while Woody Guthrie's self-titled album offered poignant folk narratives. Louis Armstrong's "Jazz Classics" and Benny Goodman Sextet's eponymous album were testaments to the enduring appeal of jazz.

Up Swing

Woody Guthrie

Jazz Classics

Benny Goodman Sextet

Meanwhile, the airwaves were filled with Bing Crosby's uplifting "Swinging On A Star" and his equally captivating "I'll Be Seeing You." Judy Garland's enchanting "Trolley Song" and Jimmy Dorsey's "Besame Mucho" added romantic flair. These songs and albums not only defined the musical identity of 1944 but also offered a respite from the uncertainties of the time, solidifying their place in the musical history of the 1940s.

Swinging On A Star

I'll Be Seeing You

Trolley Song

Besame Mucho

Top Albums 1944 (besteveralbums.com):

1. The King Cole Trio - The King Cole Trio
2. Tommy Dorsey / Glenn Miller / Benny Goodman / Artie Shaw - Up Swing
3. Woody Guthrie - Woody Guthrie
4. Louis Armstrong - Jazz Classics
5. Benny Goodman Sextet - Benny Goodman Sextet
6. Harry "The Hipster" Gibson - Boogie Woogie In Blue
7. Josh White - Josh White Sings Easy
8. Fats Waller - Favorites
9. Judy Garland - Meet Me In St. Louis
10. James P. Johnson - New York Jazz
11. Count Basie And His All-American Rhythm Section - Blues By Basie
12. Josh White - Folk Songs

 Top Singles 1944 (billboardtop100of.com):

1. Bing Crosby - Swinging On A Star
2. Judy Garland - Trolley Song
3. Jimmy Dorsey - Besame Mucho
4. Mills Brothers - You Always Hurt The One You Love
5. Merry Macs - Mairzy Doates
6. Bing Crosby - I'll Be Seeing You
7. Les Brown - Twilight Time
8. Guy Lombardo - It's Love-Love-Love
9. Glen Gray - My Heart Tells Me
10. Bing Crosby - I Love You
11. Dinah Shore - I'll Walk Alone
12. Ella Fitzgerald & Ink Spots - I'm Making Believe

♫ **Neither the Grammy Awards nor the Brit Awards existed in 1944.**

Radio

In 1944, during World War II, television was in its early stages, with most developments focused on technical advancements rather than regular programming. Consequently, radio emerged as the primary conduit of information, entertainment, and morale. It offered a diverse mix of news, drama, and music, providing comfort and connection in uncertain times. This period was characterized by groundbreaking radio broadcasts and enduring programs that reflected the era's challenges and the significant role of radio, as television had not yet become a widespread or influential medium.

Roosevelt's Wartime Address: State of the Union Fireside Chat - January 11th

State of the Union Fireside Chat

In his 1944 State of the Union address, delivered as a Fireside Chat from the White House, President Franklin D. Roosevelt presented the visionary "Second Bill of Rights," emphasizing the interconnection between economic security and true freedom. He proposed rights encompassing employment, fair wages, housing, healthcare, and education. Delivered from the White House due to illness, this address marked a significant shift towards ensuring a higher standard of living and peace, laying the groundwork for post-war America's social and economic policies.

ABSIE's Launch: Revolutionizing Wartime Radio Communication - April 30th

The American Broadcasting Station in Europe (ABSIE), a joint venture of the U.S. Office of War Information and the BBC, was vital in WWII's information

The BBC reports on D-Day operations

war. Established to counter Nazi propaganda, ABSIE began broadcasting in April 1944 from London, delivering crucial news about impending Allied actions including D-Day. Its broadcasts, reaching occupied Europe, combined musical and other programs with subtle anti-German messages. Notable artists like Bing Crosby and Dinah Shore featured in programs designed to demoralize German forces. The broadcast operations of ABSIE continued until July 1945.

Fall of Rome Fireside Chat: A Milestone in Allied Progress - June 5th

In President Roosevelt's Fireside Chat following the Fall of Rome, he celebrated this milestone while reminding the nation of the ongoing struggle against Axis powers. Roosevelt highlighted Rome's historic significance, the unified effort of Allied forces, and

FDR's Fireside Chats

the resilience of the Italian people under Fascist rule. He emphasized that Rome's liberation was more than a military triumph, reflecting a symbol of authority and culture, and marked a significant step towards achieving lasting peace and freedom from tyranny.

D-Day Normandy Landings: Radio's Historic Announcement - June 6th

Real Time Radio Broadcast Announcing D-DAY To French Resistance

The D-Day Normandy Landings were first announced to the American public through a historic radio broadcast just after midnight on June 6, 1944. Initial skepticism due to the operation's secrecy soon gave way to confirmation. President Franklin D. Roosevelt then delivered a national radio address, framing it as a prayer. He revealed his prior knowledge of the landings, underscoring their significance in liberating Europe and establishing a key Second Front. This marked a pivotal moment in World War II, significantly weakening Hitler's position between the Red Army and Allied forces.

'Ozzie and Harriet' Debut: Family Radio's Milestone - October 8th

"The Adventures of Ozzie and Harriet," a landmark family radio show, debuted on CBS in 1944. Created by Ozzie Nelson in response to Red Skelton's military drafting, it featured the real-life Nelson family. The show later moved to NBC, finally settling on ABC, where it ran until 1954. Pioneering in its seamless move from radio to television, the show initially used professional actors for sons David and Ricky, who joined the cast in 1949, replacing professional actors. Known for its entertaining content, the show also subtly countered German propaganda during WWII. It was sponsored by companies like International Silver and Heinz, reflecting the era's commercial radio landscape.

Ozzie and Harriet

RAI's Birth: Italy's Broadcasting Transformation Post-Fascism - October 26th

In October 1944, with fascism's defeat in most of Italy, the national broadcasting organization Ente Italiano per le Audizioni Radiofoniche (EIAR) underwent a significant transformation, becoming Radio Audizioni Italiane (RAI). This marked a key shift in Italian broadcasting, as the country

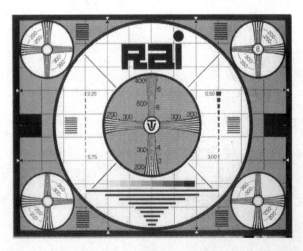

moved away from its Fascist-era media controls towards a more open and diverse media landscape. The renaming and overhaul of EIAR to RAI represented a crucial step in Italy's post-fascist evolution, ushering in a new era for Italian radio and television broadcasting.

RAI

Radio Ratings 1944 (otrcat.com)

 1943-44 Radio Programs

Program Title	Network	C.A.B. Rating
Fibber McGee & Molly	NBC	31.9
Pepsodent Program (Bob Hope)	NBC	31.6
Raleigh Cigarette Program (Red Skelton)	NBC	31.4
Chase & Sanborn Program (Edgar Bergen & Charlie McCarthy)	NBC	29.2
Grape-Nuts & Grape-Nuts Flakes Program (Jack Benny)	NBC	27.9
The Aldrich Family	NBC	26.3
Sealtest Village Store (Joan Davis)	NBC	24.2
Abbott & Costello Show	NBC	24.0
Mr. District Attorney	NBC	22.9
Maxwell House Coffee Time (Frank Morgan & Fanny Brice)	NBC	22.5

 1944-45 Radio Programs

Program Title	Network	C.A.B. Rating
Pepsodent Program (Bob Hope)	NBC	34.1
Fibber McGee & Molly	NBC	30.8
Kraft Music Hall (Bing Crosby)	NBC	25.8

The Jergens Journal (Walter Winchell)	NBC	25.3
Mr. District Attorney	NBC	25.1
Lux Radio Theater	CBS	24.5
Chase & Sanborn Program (Edgar Bergen & Charlie McCarthy)	NBC	24.2
Lucky Strike Program (Jack Benny)	NBC	24.2
Sealtest Village Store (Joan Davis)	NBC	24.0
Lady Esther Screen Guild Theater	CBS	23.4

The Primetime Emmy Awards did not exist in 1944.

Chapter IV: Sports Review 1944

American Sports

In 1944, the landscape of American sports was significantly impacted by World War II. Many sporting events were either modified or canceled due to the ongoing global conflict.

Here's an overview of key American sports events from that year, highlighting the most significant occurrences and cancellations, capturing the resilience and creativity of athletes and organizers in this challenging era.

Packers' starting offense

NFL Championship: The Green Bay Packers won against the New York Giants with a score of 14–7. The NFL continued during World War II with some team mergers due to player shortages.

College Football National Championship: The 1944 Army Cadets, representing the United States Military Academy, were a formidable force in college football, achieving a perfect 9–0 record. Their dominance, outscoring opponents 504 to 35, not only earned them national championship status but also underscored the convergence of sports and military during wartime.

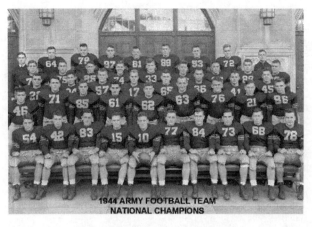

The 1944 Army Football Team

This period was part of their impressive 32-game undefeated streak, spanning from 1944 through 1946, exemplifying the team's prowess and the era's unique sports-military relationship.

Baseball - World Series: The St. Louis Cardinals defeated the St. Louis Browns, 4 games to 2 in the World Series. Additionally, the Negro World Series saw the Homestead Grays triumph over the Birmingham Black

1944 St. Louis Cardinals

Barons, 4 games to 1. Major League Baseball continued through the war years with some players serving in the military.

1944 Zollner Pistons

Basketball - NBL Championship: Fort Wayne Zollner Pistons won over the Sheboygan Redskins with a 3–0 series score. The NBA wasn't established until 1946; pre-NBA, the National Basketball League (NBL) was a significant basketball league in the U.S.

Bob Montgomery (left) v Beau Jack (right)

Boxing: At the "War Bonds Fight" on August 4, Beau Jack triumphed over Bob Montgomery in a ten-round bout that raised a record $36 million for the war effort, notably through 15,822 war bonds. The event, where tickets were donated for servicemen's use, saw both fighters, serving as privates, forgoing their purses.

Golf: Major tournaments like the Masters Tournament and U.S. Open were not played due to World War II. However, the Women's Western Open was won by Babe Zaharias.

Pensive, Kentucky Derby, 1944

Horse Racing - Triple Crown Races: Pensive won both the Kentucky Derby and Preakness Stakes, while Bounding Home won the Belmont Stakes . 71 - Pensive, Kentucky Derby, 1944

Hockey - Stanley Cup: The Montreal Canadiens swept the Chicago Black Hawks in four straight games to win the Stanley Cup, a key event in hockey, which continued through the war years.

1944 Montreal Canadiens

Tennis - American Championships: The U.S. National Championships (now the U.S. Open) continued, showcasing tennis' endurance during the war. Frank Parker and Pauline Betz Addie won the American Men's and Women's Singles Championships, respectively.

Frank Parker   Pauline Betz Addie

British Sports

The British sporting world in 1944 saw substantial alterations owing to World War II, leading to numerous event cancellations and adjustments. This recap will explore the adaptations within various sports during this tumultuous period.

Football: During 1944, the Football League, Second Division, and FA Cup were suspended in England due to World War II. Instead, regional league competitions were organized, with Tottenham Hotspur, Lovell's Athletic, Blackpool, Bath City, and Wrexham emerging as winners in various regional leagues.

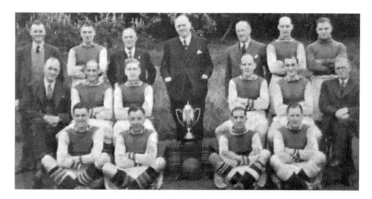

1944 Aston Villa

The Football League War Cup, a special tournament held as a substitute for the suspended national competitions, saw Aston Villa and Charlton Athletic winning the Northern and Southern sections, respectively, in a competition that drew significant public interest despite the ongoing war.

A RAAF cricket team, 1944

Cricket: All first-class cricket was canceled in the English cricket seasons from 1940 to 1944 due to World War II. However, league cricket at the one-day match level continued, with competitions like the Birmingham League, Bradford League, and Lancashire

League still active. Notable matches at Lord's included an England XI playing against "West Indies" and "Australia" teams, with England winning both matches.

Golf: The Open Championship, one of golf's major championships, was not held from 1940 to 1945 due to the Second World War.

Tennis: Wimbledon, the prestigious tennis championship, was not held in 1944 due to World War II.

Rowing: The Oxford and Cambridge Boat Race was not contested.

Rugby: Rugby League Combined services played Rugby Union Combined services, under Union laws, at Odsal (Bradford) with the league side winning 15 - 10. Bob Weighill, who later became secretary of the Rugby Football Union, played.

Wales Services v England Services Match, 1944

International Sports

In 1944, the international sports calendar was largely disrupted by World War II, leading to the cancellation of many key events and the modification of others.

Here is a synopsis of the situation across different sports.

Football: Some national leagues continued, with Valencia CF winning La Liga and Dresdner SC winning the German football championship.

However, major football competitions in England, Scotland, and France were suspended due to the war.

Valencia CF celebrates its victory, 1944

1944 Dresdner SC

Cricket: First-class cricket in England, Australia, and South Africa was not played. Some first-class matches occurred in the West Indies and New Zealand, but these were not part of any official competition.

Cycling: The Tour de France was not contested due to World War II.

Golf: Major tournaments like the Masters, U.S. Open, and British Open were not played due to the war.

Horse Racing: Prestigious races such as the Cheltenham Gold Cup, Grand National, and Champion Hurdle were not held.

Motor Racing: No major races were held worldwide due to World War II.

Olympics: Both the Winter Olympics, planned to be held in Cortina d'Ampezzo, and the Summer Olympics, scheduled in London, were cancelled.

Rugby: The New Zealand rugby league season and Northern Rugby Football League Wartime Emergency League season took place, but the Five Nations Championship series was not contested.

The Wales v South Africa game in a German stalag between prisoners of war in 1944

Speed Skating: The World Championships were not contested due to the war.

Tennis: Wimbledon and the Australian Championships were not contested, though some matches, like the French Men's and Women's Singles Championships, were still played with limited details available.

Chapter V: General 1944

Pop Culture

No Exit

"No Exit" Premiere: Sartre's Existential Impact on Theatre – May

Jean-Paul Sartre's play "No Exit," premiered at the Théâtre du Vieux-Colombier in Paris, is a seminal work in existentialist theater. The play, set in a mysterious room depicting the afterlife, explores the psychological and philosophical struggles of three characters locked together for eternity. Renowned for its famous line "Hell is other people," the play delves into themes of self-deception and the human condition, reflecting Sartre's existentialist ideas. Its original title, "Huis clos," means "behind closed doors" in French, indicating its intimate and introspective nature. The play's critical reception was positive and it remains a significant piece in modern theater.

Hitler Assassination Attempt: The 20 July Plot - July 20th

The 20 July Plot in 1944 was a significant but failed attempt by German military officers and civilians to assassinate Adolf Hitler and overthrow the Nazi regime. The conspiracy's mastermind, Claus von Stauffenberg, aimed

Bomb damage to the conference room

to kill Hitler with a bomb placed in a briefcase. The bomb exploded but only caused minor injuries to Hitler due to its positioning.

Despite the failure to kill Hitler, the plotters initiated a short-lived coup in Berlin, using Operation Valkyrie. However, the Nazi regime quickly reasserted control, leading to the execution of Stauffenberg and many other conspirators. This historical event was dramatized in the 2008 film "Valkyrie," with Tom Cruise portraying Stauffenberg.

Hitler's tattered trousers

"Appalachian Spring": Copland's Ballet Triumph - October 30th

Aaron Copland's ballet "Appalachian Spring," first performed in Washington, D.C., represents a defining moment in American ballet. The

Premiere of 'Appalachian Spring'

ballet, commissioned by arts patron Elizabeth Sprague Coolidge, won the Pulitzer Prize for music in 1945. Its narrative centers around a wedding celebration at a Pennsylvania farmhouse in the early 20th century, depicting themes of apprehension and reassurance in the lives of a young couple. Featuring Copland's iconic variations on the Shaker hymn "Simple Gifts," the ballet's music became one of the composer's most familiar works, evoking a serene yet joyous atmosphere.

Olivier's "Henry V": Shakespearean Cinema Landmark - November 22nd

Laurence Olivier's film "Henry V" marked a turning point in cinematic adaptations of Shakespeare. The film, which Olivier also directed and starred in, opened with a panoramic view of Elizabethan London and transitioned from the Globe Theatre's stage to a cinematic portrayal. Filmed during WWII in Britain and Ireland, it paralleled the 15th-century invasion of Normandy with the then-recent Allied invasion, enhancing its wartime propaganda value. Olivier received an

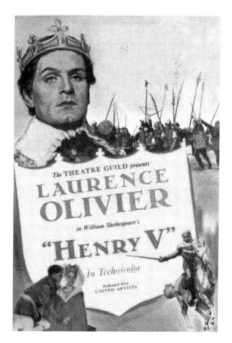

Henry V

honorary Academy Award for his multifaceted role in bringing the play to screen, and the film is lauded as one of the best Shakespeare adaptations.

Glenn Miller Missing: A Major Loss in Music History - December 15th

Chicago Daily Tribune, December 25, 1944

Glenn Miller's disappearance during a World War II flight over the English Channel was a profound loss in music history. As an acclaimed big band leader, composer, and arranger, Miller was traveling to entertain troops in France when he vanished. His Major Glenn Miller Army Air Forces Orchestra significantly influenced wartime music, while his civilian band was the top-selling recording group from 1939 to 1942, known for classics like "Moonlight Serenade." Miller was posthumously awarded the Bronze Star Medal in February 1945, and his musical legacy continues to be celebrated.

Glenn Miller Orchestra

"The Glass Menagerie": Williams' Dramatic Masterpiece - December 26th

Tennessee Williams' "The Glass Menagerie," a memory play that premiered in Chicago in 1944, marked his rise from obscurity to fame. With autobiographical elements, the play features characters mirroring Williams, his dramatic mother, and fragile sister. Originating from a short story and a screenplay titled "The Gentleman Caller," it gained traction through Chicago critics Ashton Stevens and Claudia Cassidy, leading to its Broadway success. There, it won the New York Drama Critics' Circle Award in 1945, establishing Williams as a prominent American playwright.

The Glass Menagerie

Technological Advancements

Transatlantic Airship Crossing: Aviation's Long-Distance Leap - June 1st

Transatlantic flights, traversing the Atlantic Ocean by aircraft, airships, or balloons, have evolved from daunting endeavors to routine journeys since the

A U.S. Navy K-class blimp, 1944

mid-20th century. Initially, the limited reliability and power of early aircraft engines, coupled with navigational challenges and unpredictable weather, made such flights challenging. A milestone was achieved on June 1, 1944, when two K class blimps, K-123 and K-130, from the US Navy's Blimp Squadron 14 completed the first transatlantic crossing by non-rigid airships, traveling from Massachusetts to French Morocco via Newfoundland and the Azores.

IBM's Harvard Mark I: Dawn of the Computer Era - August 7th

The Harvard Mark I, also known as the IBM Automatic Sequence Controlled Calculator (ASCC), was a pioneering electromechanical

Harvard Mark I

computer used in WWII's latter stages. Developed by IBM and operational by 1944 at Harvard, it played a key role in the Manhattan Project under John von Neumann's direction. The Mark I's computations for the atomic bomb's implosion mechanism and mathematical tables echoed Charles Babbage's 19th-century analytical engine. Fondly nicknamed "Bessy, the Bessel engine," it was later disassembled and parts are preserved at IBM, the Smithsonian, and Harvard's Science and Engineering Complex. The Mark I significantly advanced automated complex calculations in computing.

Operation Pluto: Wartime Engineering Triumph - August 12th

Operation Pluto (Pipeline Under the Ocean), a WWII British engineering feat, involved constructing submarine pipelines under the English

Laying the pipeline

Channel to support Operation Overlord. Addressing the need for fuel transport, Pluto reduced dependence on vulnerable coastal tankers. Innovations like the "Hais" and "Hamel" pipelines connected to camouflaged stations in Sandown and Dungeness. While "Bambi" from Sandown to Cherbourg was less effective, "Dumbo" from Dungeness to Boulogne succeeded, delivering 180 million imperial gallons of petrol until the war's end, accounting for 8% of Allied fuel supplies in North West Europe.

V2 Rocket Attacks: London Under Technological Siege - September

The V-2 rocket, Nazi Germany's Vergeltungswaffe 2 (Retaliation Weapon 2), the world's first long-range guided ballistic missile and artificial object to reach space, brought unprecedented terror to London. Part of Germany's vengeance for Allied bombings, over 3,000 V-2s targeted Allied cities, with London, Antwerp, and Liège bearing a significant brunt. These attacks resulted in approximately 9,000 civilian and military deaths. The supersonic V-2s, striking without

A replica of a V-2 rocket

audible warning, were unstoppable with no effective defense. Post-war, the Allied race to secure V-2 technology led to major advancements in rocketry, notably involving key German scientists like Wernher von Braun.

Hanford's Plutonium Production: Shaping Nuclear Age - November 6th

Hanford's B Reactor in operation

The Hanford Site in Washington, initiated as part of the Manhattan Project in 1943, became home to the world's first full-scale plutonium production reactor. Producing its first plutonium on November 6, 1944, its output was crucial for the first atomic bomb and the Nagasaki bombing. Expanding during the Cold War, Hanford fueled most of the U.S. nuclear arsenal, marking significant technological progress. However, early safety oversights caused environmental and health hazards. Now, Hanford's B Reactor is at the heart of a major environmental cleanup effort.

USS Archerfish vs Shinano: Submarine Warfare Milestone - November 29th

The USS Archerfish, a Balao-class submarine, achieved a significant milestone in submarine warfare by sinking the Japanese aircraft carrier Shinano in November 1944. This event marked the largest warship ever sunk by a submarine. Shinano, initially a Yamato-class super-battleship, was converted to an aircraft carrier after the Battle of Midway. Unbeknownst to U.S. intelligence, it was hastily commissioned due to fear of air attacks. Archerfish, on its maiden voyage, encountered and destroyed Shinano

USS Archerfish (SS-311)

southwest of Tokyo Bay, earning a Presidential Unit Citation for this remarkable feat.

Fashion

Fashion in 1944, shaped by the backdrop of World War II, balanced practicality and restrained style for both men and women. The war's impact was evident in the fabric rationing, design restrictions, and the influence of military clothing on civilian fashion.

African American teenagers in Zoot suits

1944 American Men's Suits

1944 Men's grey fedora hat with black band

1944 men's fashion was characterized by a sense of volume and comfort. Suits, a staple for day, sport, or evening wear, were designed to make a man feel "larger than life" despite fabric rationing. The popular Zoot Suit, with its bright colors, baggy legs, and long jackets, was a deviation from the norm, symbolizing rebellion, especially among inner-city youth. Men's clothing featured high-waisted, wide-leg trousers, wide lapel suit coats and sport coats, wide collar shirts, colorful and wide neckties, two-tone oxford shoes, and wide-brim fedora hats. These designs were a contrast to the later skinny fits of modern fashion.

World War II's restrictions on clothing in the USA, such as no flap pockets on suits, no cuffs on trousers, and selling suits without vests, influenced men's fashion. These restrictions led to innovations, like men buying longer pants to cuff them at home. In Britain, clothing restrictions were even more stringent, with no pleated backs on jackets, no metal zippers or buttons, and no raglan sleeves or half belts. The war also prompted the reuse and repurposing of clothing from the 1930s.

Women's fashion in 1944 was marked by two main silhouettes: the wedge silhouette with wide shoulders and narrow waist, often with peplum details, and the hourglass silhouette, which would become iconic with Dior's New Look in 1947. Utility clothing, with basic suits and high-waisted pants, was prevalent due to fabric restrictions. Women's wardrobes were minimalist, emphasizing frugality and versatility, with simple wedding attire and luminous buttons for blackout conditions being notable trends. The 'make-do-and-mend' approach was a necessity due to rationing and budget constraints.

Bright and colorful clothing was popular, with women's shoes often in red, white, or blue. Accessories

Wartime fashion

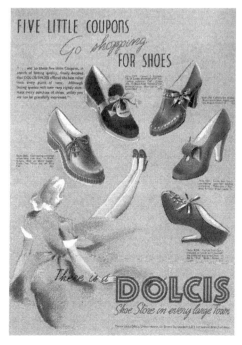

Women's Shoes

Dior's New Look in 1947

played a significant role, with gloves matching outfits being a staple for women.

In summary, 1944 fashion was a complex interplay of wartime practicality, understated glamour, and the beginnings of a shift towards more relaxed and casual styles. This period in fashion history was marked by resourcefulness and a subtle defiance against the constraints of war, setting the stage for the dramatic fashion evolutions in the subsequent decades.

Gloves, even in "Summer Styles"

Cars

The year 1944 was a decisive period for the automotive industry, deeply intertwined with the global turmoil of World War II. With a major shift from civilian to military production, the industry played a crucial role in supporting the war effort. Major automakers in the United States and the United Kingdom retooled their factories to manufacture military vehicles, equipment, and aircraft components. This era marked a significant departure from traditional car manufacturing, emphasizing the industry's adaptability and innovation in times of crisis.

Military Vehicle Production in the U.S.A.

In the U.S., 1944 was not a year of traditional car sales but of military production. The industry, comprising giants like GM, Ford, and Chrysler, focused on manufacturing vital war materials, contributing 20% to the total U.S. output for the war effort. General Motors was a significant contributor, producing goods worth $12 billion, equating to 41% of the industry's output and 8% of the entire American war economy. Ford followed with contributions of $3.9 billion,

1944 Willys MB Jeep

while Chrysler was close behind with $3.5 billion in war contracts. Notable productions included military vehicles such as trucks, armored cars, and tanks.

Boeing B-29 Superfortress

The iconic Willys MB Jeep was a key figure in this arsenal, known for its robustness and versatility. Ford and GM also produced warplanes, and Chrysler was involved in manufacturing parts for the B-29 bomber, a significant contribution to the air warfare segment.

British Automotive Industry's War Effort

The British automotive industry, similar to its American counterpart, pivoted towards military production. The sector transformed to produce a

Tilly car

79

range of military vehicles, including tanks, staff cars, and utility vehicles like the Tilly car.

Powered by a Bristol Mercury engine

Manufacturers like Morris, Austin, and Daimler reorganized to support the Allied war effort, contributing to the dramatic increase in military vehicles. Austin, in particular, manufactured aircraft components for Bristol Mercury radial engines and assembled thousands of aircraft, including Lancaster Bombers. Daimler produced armored cars and scout cars, and also contributed significantly to aircraft parts production.

Lancaster Bomber

Key Military Vehicles of 1944

The most prominent military vehicle of 1944 was the Willys MB Jeep. Designed for reconnaissance and utility, the Jeep became an emblem of American military prowess. Its adaptability and resilience made it indispensable in various military operations across different terrains, contributing significantly to the success of Allied forces. Other notable military vehicles included the GMC CCKW cargo truck and the M4 Sherman tank, which played crucial roles in logistics and armored warfare, respectively.

Willys MB Jeep

GMC CCKW cargo truck

M4 Sherman tank

Innovations in Automotive Technology

The war period saw significant innovations in automotive technology, largely driven by military needs. These advancements included enhanced four-wheel-drive systems, advanced suspension technologies, and improvements in diesel engines for heavy vehicles. The development of these technologies during the war laid the foundation for post-war automotive advancements, influencing future civilian vehicle design and functionality.

Impact on Post-War Automotive Design

The conclusion of World War II in 1945 set the stage for a resurgence in the automotive industry. The technological advancements and manufacturing techniques developed during the war heavily influenced post-war automotive design. This period witnessed the introduction of more streamlined car designs, the adoption of advanced engineering techniques, and an increase in production efficiencies, shaping the future of the automotive industry.

Critical Contribution to the War Effort

The automotive industry's contribution to the war effort was monumental. Automakers played a critical role in producing a wide range of military equipment, from vehicles to aircraft and weapon components. This massive production effort was vital to the Allied victory and showcased the industry's capacity for rapid innovation and scaled-up production in response to global crises.

Popular Recreation

In 1944, a year deeply entrenched in the throes of World War II, the landscape of popular recreation was markedly shaped by the conflict, with entertainment and leisure activities serving as crucial escapes from the hardships of wartime.

Radio was the primary source of news and entertainment, with its popularity soaring during the war. Nearly ten million radio licenses were issued

Family time

in Britain by 1945. The BBC, with its near-monopoly, offered a range of shows, from the informative "Brains Trust" to popular comedy such as "It's That Man Again." The beloved singer Vera Lynn, known as the 'Forces Sweetheart,' hosted her radio program, "Sincerely Yours – Vera Lynn," where she sang and relayed messages to troops overseas from their families.

Cinema was a significant pastime, with weekly ticket sales in Britain between 25 and 30 million. Despite being released earlier, "Gone With The Wind" and British films like "In Which We Serve" and "Millions Like Us" remained major hits in 1944. They continued to draw audiences for their escapism from the hardships of wartime and their cultural relevance, reflecting the experiences and struggles of the era, especially given the scarcity of new film releases due to the war.

The Brains Trust

The ITMA cast at rehearsal, January 1944

Vera Lynn broadcasting

Gone With The Wind   In Which We Serve

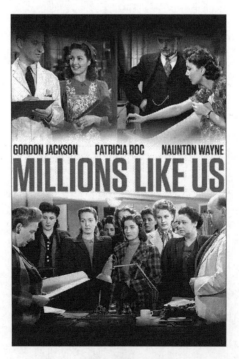

In Which We Serve

1940s Matinée photo

Theatre played a vital role in providing cultural relief. Although initially closed at the outbreak of war, many theatres soon reopened with matinées or early evening performances. The Council for the Encouragement of Music and the Arts (CEMA) supported the arts by organizing concerts featuring classical music and drama, bringing ballet and opera to new audiences.

Pianist Myra Hess

Notably, the National Gallery in London hosted a series of lunchtime concerts throughout the war, featuring celebrated pianist Myra Hess and other classical performers.

Professional sports, particularly football, were significantly impacted by the war. Football grounds reopened in September 1944 with reorganized leagues to minimize travel and restricted crowd sizes. Despite many players being called up into the forces and the damage to grounds by bombing, spectators still attended matches in these reformatted leagues.

Pubs also faced challenges due to reduced supplies of sugar and grain for brewing beer and whisky. The erratic supply of beer led many patrons to change their habits, visiting pubs during weeknights or early evenings.

The Cricketers, Brighton, 1944: Mrs Pitt pours a beer

Vintage Cast Iron Curtiss P-40 Warhawk Toy

Supermarine Spitfire Toy

In the realm of toys and games, due to the war effort, few toys were sold in the early 1940s as materials like steel and rubber were needed for producing military equipment. However, World War II model plane kits were popular among children, featuring models such as the Curtiss Warhawk P-40 and the Supermarine Spitfire. Tiddledy Winks/Tiddlywinks also remained a favorite, offering a simple yet engaging pastime.

The year 1944 in popular recreation thus reflected the era's complexities and the resilience of the human spirit in seeking joy and distraction amidst adversity. From radio shows to cinema, theatre performances to sports, and the simplicity of board games, these activities offered much-needed respite and a semblance of normalcy in a world disrupted by war. They stood as testaments

Tiddlywinks

to the enduring power of entertainment and leisure in sustaining morale and fostering a sense of community during one of history's most challenging periods.

Chapter VI: Births & Deaths 1944

Births (onthisday.com)

January 9th – Jimmy Page: English Rock Guitarist

January 12th – Joe Frazier: American Boxer

January 18th – Paul Keating: Australian Politician

January 19th – Peter Lynch: American Investor

February 8th – Sebastião Salgado: Brazilian Photographer

February 9th – Alice Walker: American Novelist

February 14th – Alan Parker: English Film Director

February 22nd – Robert Kardashian: American attorney and businessman

February 29th – Dennis Farina: American Actor

March 1st – Roger Daltrey: English Singer

March 17th – Pattie Boyd: English Model and Photographer

March 26th – Diana Ross: American Singer and Actress

April 18th – Robert Hanssen: American FBI Agent

May 6th – Masanori Murakami: Japanese Baseball Player

May 14th – George Lucas: American Film Director

May 20th – Joe Cocker: English Rock Vocalist

May 23rd – John Newcombe: Australian Tennis Player

May 25th – Frank Oz: American Puppeteer

May 28th – Gladys Knight: American Singer

May 28th – Rudy Giuliani: American Politician

June 6th – Tommie Smith: American Athlete

June 19th – Chico Buarque: Brazilian Singer-Songwriter

June 24th – Jeff Beck: English Guitarist

July 13th – Ernő Rubik: Hungarian Inventor

August 7th – John Glover: American Actor

August 17th – Larry Ellison: American Businessman

August 19th – Jack Canfield: American Author

August 20th – Rajiv Gandhi: Indian Politician

September 12th – Barry White: American Singer

September 16th – Ard Schenk: Dutch Speed Skater

September 25th – Michael Douglas: American Actor

October 4th – Tony La Russa: American Baseball Manager

November 10th – Tim Rice: British Lyricist

November 10th – Tim Rice: British Lyricist

December 3rd – António Variações: Portuguese Singer-Songwriter

December 22nd – Steve Carlton: American Baseball Player

Deaths (onthisday.com)

January 23rd – Edvard Munch: Norwegian Painter

February 1st – Piet Mondrian: Dutch Abstract Painter

February 23rd – Leo Baekeland: Belgian-American Chemist

March 4th – Louis Buchalter: American Mobster

April 29th – Billy Bitzer: American Cinematographer

April 30th – Paul Poiret: French Fashion Designer

July 12th – Theodore Roosevelt Jr.: American Military Leader

July 26th – Reza Shah Pahlavi: Shah of Iran

July 31st – Antoine de Saint-Exupéry: French Writer and Aviator

August 1st – Manuel L. Quezon: Filipino Politician

August 12th – Joseph P. Kennedy Jr.: American Naval Aviator

September 13th – Noor Inayat Khan: British Resistance Agent

September 19th – Guy Gibson: British Aviator

October 26th – Princess Beatrice: British Royal

November 25th – Kenesaw Mountain Landis: American Judge and MLB Commissioner

November 26th – Florence Foster Jenkins: American Soprano

November 30th – Albert B. Fall: American Politician

December 3rd – Prince Andrew of Greece and Denmark

December 13th – Wassily Kandinsky: Russian Painter and Art Theorist

December 14th – Lupe Vélez: Mexican Actress

December 15th – Glenn Miller: American Bandleader

December 27th – Amy Beach: American Pianist and Composer

Chapter VII: Statistics 1944

* U.S. GDP 1944 – 224 billion USD (thebalancemoney.com)

* U.S. GDP 2022 – 25.46 trillion USD (worldbank.org)

* U.K. GDP 1944 – 29.3 billion USD (worldbank.org)

* U.K. GDP 2022 – 3.07 trillion USD (worldbank.org)

* U.S. Inflation 1944 – 2.27% (officialdata.org)

* U.S. Inflation 2022 – 8.0% (worldbank.org)

* U.K. Inflation 1944 – 2.75% (officialdata.org)

* U.K. Inflation 2022 – 7.9% (worldbank.org)

* U.S. Population 1944 – 134,075,000 (countryeconomy.com)

* U.S. Population 2022 - 333,287,557 (worldbank.org)

* U.K. Population 1944 – 39,984,721 (macrotrends.net)

* U.K. Population 2022 - 66,971.41 (worldbank.org)

* U.S. Life Expectancy at Birth 1944 – 65.25 (ssa.gov)

* U.S. Life Expectancy at Birth 2022 - 79.05 (ssa.gov)

* U.K. Life Expectancy at Birth 1944 – 68.37 (ons.gov.uk)

* U.K. Life Expectancy at Birth 2022 – 81.65 (ons.gov.uk)

* U.S. Annual Working Hours Per Worker 1944 - 1,989 (ourworldindata.org)

* U.S. Annual Working Hours Per Worker 2017 - 1,757 (ourworldindata.org)

* U.K. Annual Working Hours Per Worker 1944 - 2,437 (ourworldindata.org)

* U.K. Annual Working Hours Per Worker 2017 - 1,670 (ourworldindata.org)

* U.S. Unemployment Rate 1944 – 1.2% (thebalancemoney.com)

* U.S. Unemployment Rate 2022 – 3.6% (worldbank.org)

* U.K. Unemployment Rate 1944 – 0.6% (ons.gov.uk)

* U.K. Unemployment Rate 2022 – 3.7% (ons.gov.uk)

* U.S. Tax Revenue (% of GDP) 1944 – 19.09% (taxfoundation.org)

* U.S. Tax Revenue (% of GDP) 2021 – 11.2% (worldbank.org)

* U.K. Tax Revenue (% of GDP) 1944 – 39.12% (ceicdata.com)

* U.K. Tax Revenue (% of GDP) 2021 – 26.4% (worldbank.org)

* U.S. Prison Population 1944 – 132,456 (bjs.ojp.gov)

* U.S. Prison Population 2021 - 1,204,300 (bjs.ojp.gov)

* U.K. Prison Population 1944 - 21,567 (parliament.uk)

* U.K. Prison Population 2022 - 81,806 (gov.uk)

* U.S. Average Cost of a New House 1944 – $6,384 (cnbc.com)

* U.S. Average Cost of a New House 2022 – $454,900 (gobankingrates.com)

* U.K. Average Cost of a New House 1944 – £1,123 (sunlife.co.uk)

* U.K. Average Cost of a New House 2022 – £296,000 (ons.gov.uk)

* U.S. Average Income per Year 1944 – $2,500 (census.gov)

* U.S. Average Income per Year US – $56,368 (demandsage.com)

* U.K. Average Income per Year 1944 – £477,00 (gov.uk)

* U.K. Average Income per Year 2022 – £33,000 (gov.uk)

* U.S. Cost of Living: The $100 from 1944 has grown to about $1,744.61 today, up $1,644.61 over 79 years due to an average yearly inflation of 3.69%, resulting in a 1,644.61% total price hike (in2013dollars.com).

* U.K. Cost of Living: Today's £5,468.53 mirrors the purchasing power of £100 in 1944, showing a £5,368.53 hike over 79 years. The pound's yearly inflation rate averaged 5.20% during this period, leading to a 5,368.53% total price rise (in2013dollars.com).

Cost Of Things

United States

* Men's suit, Stein Bloch: $50.00-60.00/each (mclib.info)
* Men's shoes, Nunn-Bush: $10.00-13.50/pair (mclib.info)
* Women's dress, cotton and seersucker: $8.98-12.95/each (mclib.info)
* Women's handbags: $7.50-13.95/each (mclib.info)
* Infant's dresses: $1.79/each (mclib.info)
* Fresh eggs (1 dozen): $0.55 (stacker.com)
* White bread (1 pound): $0.09 (stacker.com)
* Sliced bacon (1 pound): $0.41 (stacker.com)
* Potatoes (10 pounds): $0.47 (stacker.com)
* Fresh delivered milk (1/2 gallon): $0.31 (stacker.com)
* Apples, Rome: $0.23/2 lbs (mclib.info)
* Butter, Louctta: $0.49/lb (mclib.info)
* Tuna, canned: $0.26/6 oz can (mclib.info)
* Cereal, Kellogg's Corn Flakes: $0.08/11 oz package (mclib.info)
* Onions, Yellow no. 1: $0.28/3 lbs (mclib.info)

- ★ Oranges, Florida large sweet: $0.53/8 lb bag (mclib.info)

- ★ Peanut butter, Sultana: $0.21/lb jar (mclib.info)

- ★ Pineapples, fresh whole: $0.20/each (mclib.info)

- ★ Tomatoes: $0.10/19 oz can (mclib.info)

- ★ Soda, Coca Cola: $0.05/bottle (mclib.info)

United Kingdom (retrowow.co.uk)

- ★ Flour: 6d for a 5 Pound bag (thepeoplehistory.com)

- ★ Campbell's Tomato Soup: 6d for 3 cans (thepeoplehistory.com)

- ★ Oatmeal: 3½d (1½p) per lb (mentalscoop.com)

- ★ Sugar: 4d (1½p) per lb (mentalscoop.com)

- ★ Ivory Soap: 2d per bar (thepeoplehistory.com)

- ★ Margarine: 4½d per Pound (thepeoplehistory.com)

- ★ Milk: 9d (3½p) per quart (mentalscoop.com)

- ★ Cheese: 1/1 (5½p) per lb (mentalscoop.com)

- ★ Bacon: 1/10½ (9p) per lb (mentalscoop.com)

- ★ Eggs large: 1/9 (8½p) per dozen (mentalscoop.com)

- ★ Bread: 9d (3½p) per 4lb loaf (mentalscoop.com)

- ★ Oranges: 2d per pound (thepeoplehistory.com)

- ★ Potatoes: 9½d for 10 pounds (thepeoplehistory.com)

- ★ Rowntree's Cocoa: 6d (2½p) per ¼lb (mentalscoop.com)

- ★ Chappie Dog Food: 7d (3p) per tin (mentalscoop.com)

- ★ Black Cat Cigarettes: 10 for 6d (2½p) (mentalscoop.com)

- ★ Maltesers: 2d (1p) per packet, 6d (2½p) per box (mentalscoop.com)

Chapter VIII: Iconic Advertisements of 1944

Prestone Anti-Freeze

Philip Morris

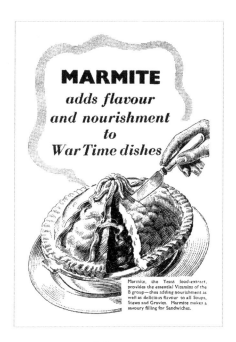

Marmite

Pan American World Airways

Cadillac

Lucky Strike

Heinz Beans

Winchester

Johnnie Walker

Kodak

Palmolive

7 Up

Havoline Motor Oil at Texaco Dealers

Marlboro

Campbell's Vegetable Soup

American Airlines

Smirnoff Vodka

Bell Telephone System

Listerine Shaving Cream

Coca-Cola

Goodyear

Chesterfield

Kellogg's Cereals

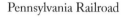

Pennsylvania Railroad

Budweiser

General Electric FM Radio

Colgate Ribbon Dental Cream

De Soto Cars

Camels

Firestone

I have a gift for you!

Dear reader, thank you so much for reading my book!

To make this book more (much more!) affordable, all images are in black and white, but I've created a special gift for you!

You can now have access, for FREE, to the PDF version of this book with the original images!

Keep in mind that some are originally black and white, but some are colored.

I hope you enjoy it!

Download it here:

bit.ly/41PqXuR

Or Scan this QR Code:

I have a favor to ask you!

I deeply hope you've enjoyed reading this book and felt transported right into 1944!

I loved researching it, organizing it, and writing it, knowing that it would make your day a little brighter.

If you've enjoyed it too, I would be extremely grateful if you took just a few minutes to leave a positive customer review and share it with your friends.

As an unknown author, that makes all the difference and gives me the extra energy I need to keep researching, writing, and bringing joy to all my readers. Thank you!

Best regards,
Charles A. Thompson

Please leave a positive book review here:

amzn.to/48vPkQM

Or Scan this QR Code:

Discover All the Books in This Collection!

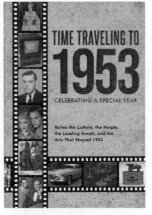

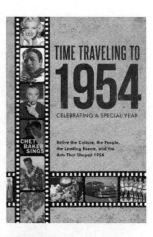

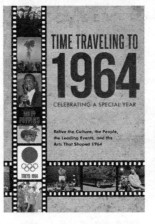

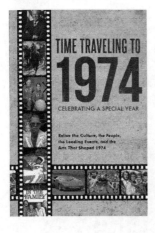

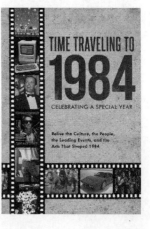

Made in the USA
Las Vegas, NV
02 December 2024

13222658R00061